Law and Society
Volume 1

Criminological Theory
Just the Basics

Volume 1
Criminological Theory. Just the Basics
Robert Heiner

Volume 2
Is Legal Reasoning Irrational?
An Introduction to the Epistemology of Law
John Woods

Law and Society Series Editors
Robert Heiner   rheiner@plymouth.edu
John Woods   john.woods@ubc.ca

Law and Society Series Editorial Board:
Malin Akerstrom, Matthias Armgardt, Donald Black, Larry
Laudan, Sebastien Magnier, Henry Prakken, Shahid Rahman,
Antonino Rotolo, Vincenzo Ruggiero, Giovanni Sartor,
Uri Schild.

Criminological Theory
Just the Basics

Robert Heiner
Plymouth State University

ISBN 978-1-84890-174-2

College Publications
Scientific Director: Dov Gabbay
Managing Director: Jane Spurr

http://www.collegepublications.co.uk

Original cover design by Laraine Welch
Printed by Lightning Source, Milton Keynes, UK

Table of Contents

Introduction

This book is aimed primarily at undergraduate students enrolled in criminology, criminal justice, and sociology courses. This introduction is aimed at their instructors. My goal with this text is to provide an alternative to the traditional way that criminological theory is treated in textbooks. Theory is usually covered in a large segment of a large criminology textbook, or in a textbook devoted exclusively to criminological theory. Either way, typically, theories are explained, as well as their evolution, their classification, their relationship to other theories, and their resilience to empirical testing. While this text does get into such discussions occasionally, when they are particularly relevant to understanding a theory, it does not cover them systematically in the presentation of each theory. These discussions of evolution, classification and the like are all important to us academics, but not so much so for students being introduced to the field of criminology or the sociology of deviance. By all means, graduate students in criminology and criminal justice should be aware of these details, and so should undergrads who are taking a course specifically in criminological theory; but undergrads in an introductory class often get bogged down in these details and, rather than learning to appreciate theory, they often learn something quite the opposite. Convinced of this, I studiously avoided—with a few exceptions—discussions of how the theories contained in this text are related to one another historically, theoretically, or philosophically. I also avoided—again, with a few exceptions—critiquing the theories contained herein.

While some treatments of criminological theory often go into too much depth, others cover too much breadth. These often describe a half a dozen or so genres of theory, each containing several theories, with each theory described in only a paragraph or two. Such treatments are also likely to be mind-boggling for a great many undergraduates, again leaving them with a distaste for theory.

The history of criminology has provided us with a wealth of insightful and tantalizing theories and it is not beyond the capability of most undergraduates to learn to appreciate them. Most treatments of theory for undergraduates, however, have not lent themselves to such an appreciation. The goal of this brief text is to provide undergraduates a tool to help them learn the *essence* of the theories that are so well-known to almost all criminologists and to acquire an appreciation for criminological theory in general.

With appreciation of theory as a goal, though I have tried to boil the classics down to their essentials, I did occasionally discuss how classical theories have been elaborated upon since their introduction. Thus, the chapter on Marx and conflict theory, for example, discusses permutations of Marxist analysis that have come along since his time. These elaborations highlight Marx's influence on subsequent theory. They should introduce important topics for class discussion and make classic theories more relevant today's students.

With a few exceptions, entries in this volume are headed by the theorists' names rather than the names of the theories. In deciding whether to employ the theorist or the theory as the heading, I was guided by my sense of which would be more familiar to most criminologists. More often than not, when criminologists address students and other criminologists, the name of the theorist becomes shorthand for the theory that is being referenced, both in their classes and in their professional writing. Two, of the entries, however—those on social disorganization theory and labeling theory—are headed by the names of the theories because there were so many theorists who contributed directly to their development, with no one theorist standing out.

Many treatments of criminological theory cover a token biological theory or two and a token psychological theory. This is often meant to demonstrate the history and evolution of criminological thought. This, however, is not my intent. I did not cover Lombroso and barely touched on Freud, for examples, because, as important as they may have been, I do not feel that they have much to contribute to the understanding of crime today. I feel that the theorists covered in this text are classics; and they are classic, not because of the role they played in the development of criminology, but because they are still relevant to the understanding of modern day crime.

The reader may note that the last theory contained in this volume was developed in 1979, more than thirty years ago. This is because for a theory to be "classic," it must survive the test of time. Certainly, interesting criminological theories have been posited since 1979; but it remains to be seen which will survive the time test. The criminological community will decide. While time-tested, no one theory contained in this small text explains all or most crime, but taken together, they explain a great deal of crime.

There is another intended audience for this basic theory primer and that consists of all of the professionals who work with or for alleged and convicted criminals: from police officers to prison guards, social workers and counselors, defense attorneys, and even judges. Many of them have had some criminological training; I venture to guess that a great many have not. But their effectiveness at their work could only be improved by at least some exposure to the very impressive body of literature on the causes of crime that has evolved over the centuries. I can easily imagine a modern day defense attorney, familiar with the works of Cesare Beccaria, invoking his name in his client's defense, as did John Quincy Adams in 1770, in his successful defense of the British officer and soldiers alleged to have been involved in the Boston Massacre.[1]

There are several people I want to thank for making this book possible. Most importantly, my thanks go to Jane Spurr, the Managing Director at College Publications. She lives and works 3,000 miles across the pond and I have never met her. This makes it all the more a mystery to me as to how she is able to get so much work done and still respond to my questions and concerns often within minutes of my e-mail. I cannot see her face when she responds; but it always seems to me that she's smiling. I also want to acknowledge my co-editor of the *Law and Society Series* at College Publications, John Woods. He lives 3,000 miles in the other direction and I can tell from our correspondence that he is a dedicated and proficient scholar who is very concerned about his students' welfare. I know it will be a delight working with him. I want to thank my colleague and friend, David Mackey, for going over the manuscript and offering many useful suggestions which, no doubt, improved the quality of the book. Lastly, I want to thank my brother, Steven Heiner, who listened to me talk about the project for months and months, read the manuscript, and also provided me with very useful feedback.

1

Cesare Beccaria

On Crimes and Punishments[1]
1764

Cesare Beccaria was born into the Italian aristocracy and
sent off for Jesuit training at the age of eight. He
resented the stifling and inflexible education among the
Jesuits. Later, he went on to the University of Pavia,
where his performance was less than impressive.
According to one biographer, "All that these years
seemed to create in the frustrated young man was
lethargy and discontent."[2] He lived in poverty for a brief
period when, over a dispute, he lost his father's financial
support. Before the publication of his treatise, *Dei delitti
e delle pene* (*On Crimes and Punishments*) in 1764,
Beccaria did little to distinguish himself from his
contemporaries and was likely considered something of
a ne'er-do-well. When he did dedicate himself to his
writing project, he spent a mere nine months working
on it and he produced one of the most important
documents in the history of Western jurisprudence.

On Crimes and Punishments was a tightly argued
attack on the use of the criminal justice system as a
means of political oppression by European aristocracies

of his time. The law of his day was used by kings, popes, and magistrates to torture, vanquish, and annihilate their enemies, and to intimidate their would-be political foes. Little or no evidence was required and there was little or nothing that we would consider judicial oversight. Because of these conditions, it was actually quite daring of Beccaria to publish his work; and it was initially published anonymously. Upon publication, however, when his name was revealed, Beccaria became an overnight sensation, hailed throughout European society as the guiding light of criminal justice reform.

Beccaria's treatise reflected the works of social contract theorists before him, especially that of the 17th century Scottish philosopher Thomas Hobbes. Social contract theorists had been interested in the question "why is there government?" This is a timelessly interesting question because where there is government (that is, everywhere), the people are not free; they are *governed*. So why do people allow themselves to be governed? According to Hobbes, without government, life would be "solitary, poor, nasty, brutish and short." That is, without government, people would be tearing at each other's throats, trying to survive or get ahead. So government arose to protect each person from every other person. A contract involves each party giving something in order to receive something in return from the other party. In this case, each individual member of a society gives up a portion of his or her freedom to form a government in order to receive protection from that government, as depicted in the figure below.[3]

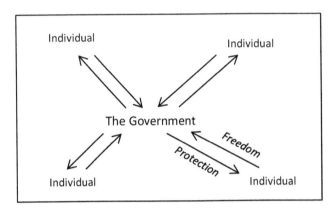

Figure 1.1: Thomas Hobbes' Social Contract

The total sum of those freedoms equals the power of the state and, *according to Beccaria, the social contract stipulates that the government can only use that power in order to protect each person from every other person. Any other use of that power constitutes a violation of the social contract.* Thus, when government officials use their power to suppress their opponents, their actions represent a violation of the social contract. Following this logic, Beccaria acknowledged the need for law and for punishments specified by the law, as these are needed to protect each person from every other person. But these need to be applied equally because we have all given equally of our freedom to form a government.

Beccaria is recognized as being a member of the **classical school of criminology**. *The classical theorists* *viewed humans as rational beings who mentally weigh the benefits and the costs of their actions. If the benefits of illegal activity outweigh the costs, then crime will be the result.* According to Beccaria, then, the state should apply only enough punishment to make crime irrational; any more than that is a violation of the social contract. In this sense, he advocated for milder forms of punishment than were prevalent in his time. Beccaria writes,

> Can the shrieks of a wretch recall from time, which never reverses its course, deeds already accomplished? The purpose can only be to prevent the criminal from inflicting new injuries on its citizens and to deter others from similar acts. . . . . *For punishment to attain its end, the evil which it inflicts has only to exceed the advantage derivable from the crime;* in this excess of evil one should include the certainty of punishment and the loss of the good which the crime might have produced.[4]

Punishments which are more severe than necessary to deter crime are not only a violation of the social contract, but they can also make crime rational as criminals "are driven to commit additional crimes to avoid punishment for a single one."[5]

Further, Beccaria argued punishment should be swift and certain because swiftness and certainty reinforce the automatic association between crime and punishment in the minds of the offender and of the public. By the same token, he opposed the granting of clemency and pardons (and by implication, probation and parole) because these weaken the association between crime and punishment. But, he notes, "As punishments become more mild, clemency and pardon become less necessary."[6]

Beccaria was a staunch opponent of torture and the death penalty, both of which were common at the time. With regards to torture, he writes,

> The fact of the crime is either certain or uncertain; if certain, all that is due is the punishment established by the laws, and tortures are useless because the criminal's confession is useless; if uncertain, then one must not torture the innocent, for such, according to the laws, is a man whose crimes are not yet proved.[7]

As for the death penalty, he argued that the intensity of punishment is less of a deterrent than its duration. The moment of death lasts just an instant and nobody knows what happens afterwards. Some even wish for death as evidenced by suicide rates which are often higher than homicide rates. But nobody wishes for a lifetime of forced labor. *The death penalty, he argued, sets an "example of barbarity"* and encourages the exact behavior that it is supposed to discourage. It is absurd, he argued, to order a public murder in order to deter murder.

There are few ideas that are original in Beccaria's treatise, but he audaciously brought these ideas together under a framework of social contract theory which appealed to his contemporaries and leading figures during the Enlightenment. Responding to the book and addressing Beccaria, Jeremy Bentham, another classical criminologist, proclaimed "Oh, my master, first evangelist of Reason . . . you who have made so many useful excursions into the path of utility, what is there left for us to do? – Never to turn aside from that path."[8] Six years after its publication, John Adams opened his defense of the soldiers involved in the Boston Massacre with a passage from Beccaria's treatise. Given that *On Crimes and Punishments* was a must-read for political reformers of his day, there is little doubt that Beccaria provided both moral and intellectual inspiration behind the both the American and French Revolutions; and his ideas are quite pronounced in the Bill of Rights of the U.S. Constitution with its emphasis on the rights of the accused. Centuries later, experts agree that Beccaria's work had "more practical effect than any other treatise ever written in the long campaign against barbarism in criminal law and procedure."[9]

2

Karl Marx

Conflict Theory
1867

Karl Marx was born in Germany of Jewish parents in 1818. Probably in response to the anti-Semitism of the times, his father converted to Christianity and Karl was baptized at the age of six. He studied law and philosophy at the University of Berlin. He began contributing articles on social and economic issues to a newspaper in Cologne and eventually became its editor. Soon he married and moved to Paris where he became involved with members of the communist movement. He found many of their ideas to be crude and impractical, but he empathized with them and was attracted to their spirit of brotherhood. His writings turned decidedly revolutionary and Marx was banished from a number of European countries. He settled in London and devoted himself to his writing. His writing would go on to become among the most influential and controversial works in history, spreading revolutionary zeal among the working classes and fear among elites throughout much of the world. Marx had very little to say about crime, *per se*;

but his ideas about the connections between politics and economics would be applied to the understanding of crime by scores of criminologists who followed him.

Marx saw the contours of history as reflecting the dynamics between competing interest groups. Writing in the early days of the Industrial Revolution, he was primarily interested in the conflict between the people who owned the factories and the people who worked for them (as discussed below); however, modern *conflict theorists* are concerned with the conflict between all interest groups: between rich and poor, men and women, blacks and whites, Christians and Muslims, etc.

Das Kapital[1] (*Capital*) was first published in 1867. It was largely a critique of capitalism, a system where the elite are allowed to accumulate wealth and power and use them at the expense of the poor. At the time, more and more labor was increasingly devoted to industrial production. People were moving out of the countryside into the cities to perform the only work available in the factories. Marx located the most pressing social problems of the day as being rooted in the relationship between factory owners (the *bourgeoisie*) and the people who worked for them (the *proletariat*). The terms of this relationship were entirely dictated by the bourgeoisie. Working conditions were abysmal—work was dangerous, hours were long, and wages were small. The proletariat had no choice but to accept these conditions, or starve. A government that represented the interests of the vast majority of its people would regulate these conditions; but, instead, the government represented the interests of the bourgeoisie and allowed such conditions to continue.

According to Marx, in a capitalist economy, the difference between what the worker is worth and what the worker is paid is equal to profit. In other words, the employer makes a profit by paying his or her employees less than what they are worth. This is a system based solely on exploitation and, according to Marx, such a system depends upon the maintenance of relatively high levels of unemployment. When unemployment rates are high, workers compete more fiercely for jobs, making them willing to accept lower wages, and increasing the profits for their employers. Again, a government that represented the interests of the people would ensure the welfare of the unemployed, but such "interference" in the economy would weaken the sting of unemployment, competition for jobs would become less fierce, wages would go up, and the profits of the bourgeoisie would go down. Instead, a government that represented the interests of the elite would ensure that the unemployed are allowed to suffer.

This is the jumping off point for many of the conflict criminologists who followed in the Marxist tradition, noting, for example, that most of the people in prison today were poor and unemployed before they got there. Many modern conflict theorists, or *critical criminologists*, focus their attention on the United States because it has one of the most capitalistic economies and does way less to moderate the pains of poverty and unemployment than most other industrialized nations, ostensibly because such moderating policies constitute "interference" in the free market economy. Consequently, *the United States has relatively high rates of inequality and poverty, and the highest incarceration rate in the world.*

When an economy requires high rates of unemployment, there is need to deal with the millions of "surplus" population. This population, according to Steven Spitzer[2], falls into two categories: social junk and social dynamite. *Social junk* is made up of the elderly and disabled as well as millions of unemployed people who accept current economic arrangements and are biding their time until a new job comes along. *Social dynamite* is made up of those who do not accept current economic arrangements and, therefore, pose a threat to the status quo. The United States spends tens of billions of dollars a year to neutralize the social dynamite through its criminal justice system, in particular, its system of incarceration; and tens of billions more are spent through its welfare system, providing financial assistance to the social junk, just enough to prevent them from transforming into social dynamite. *All of this time, money and effort are spent to control the unemployed and preserve the status quo which benefits elite interests to the detriment of the working class.*

Not only do the elite dictate the terms of the relationship between employers and their employees, but they also have substantial influence over the crafting of legislation, that is, in defining what is "criminal" and who gets punished and how. This is where the study of white collar crime comes into play. Until Edwin Sutherland introduced the concept of the "white collar criminal" in 1940[3] (see Chapter 6), criminologists focused all of their attention on crimes committed by the poor. Sutherland, instead, demonstrated that many, if not most, of the largest, most reputable corporations in the United States routinely engaged in criminal activity with virtual impunity. Since then, *criminologists have frequently argued that the harms done by corporations and white collar criminals far outweigh the harms done by poor criminals.* This goes for both financial harm (insider trading, collusion, and the financial maneuverings that led to trillions of dollars in losses during the Great Recession starting in 2008) as well a physical harm (pollution, the sale of dangerous products, unsafe working conditions). And yet, the law has been crafted in such a way that the crimes committed by the elite do not fit a legal standard for "crime;" or they are dealt with in civil or regulatory courts where the punishments or less severe; or when they do receive criminal convictions, white collar criminals are often sent to minimum security prisons where the "pains of imprisonment" are less severe.

Lastly the elite have substantial influence over the dissemination and content of the information that we receive. Through their ownership of media outlets, they can exercise such control. But even when they do not have control through ownership, the elite can influence media content through advertising dollars, because advertising makes up most or all of the revenue for most media outlets. That is, news media outlets do not want to run afoul of elite interests because, if they were to do so, their advertising revenue would vanish. Therefore, *given prevailing patterns of news coverage, the public comes to perceive that the real threat of crime is posed by the poor and not by the rich.* We are also led to believe the poor are slovenly and inclined to take advantage of welfare assistance. According to the critical criminologists, the real "enemy" of both the lower and middle classes is the disproportionate influence that elite interests have over their living conditions. But *the fear and distrust of the poor propagated by the media prevents the oppressed classes from realizing their common interests and uniting to fight for a more fair and just society.*

3

Emile Durkheim

Functionalism
1895

Emile Durkheim was born in Epinal, France in 1858. His father, grandfather and great-grandfather had been rabbis and the same was expected of him; but he rejected Judaism in his youth. He aspired to become a teacher and he studied at the prestigious L'école Normale Supérieure. Upon completing his studies, he took on successive teaching posts and he was appointed to the faculty of the University of Paris in 1906. As an early advocate for the scientific study of society and human behavior, Durkheim attracted some opposition among his contemporaries who were more philosophically-minded. The social scientific perspective was and still is controversial because it takes a more deterministic view of human behavior while downplaying the role of free will. Durkheim was instrumental in getting sociology established as an academic discipline. He wrote about numerous subjects including, the division of labor, suicide, education and religion. His works have become enduring classics and he is often cited in contemporary sociology and criminology classes as well as in a variety of other disciplines.

Durkheim became the most influential proponent of a branch of sociology called **functionalism**. Before Durkheim, the British philosopher Herbert Spencer compared society to a living organism, a system of interdependent parts, evolving and struggling to maintain stability. Durkheim did not take the living organism analogy literally, but he did make extensive use of the logic of that analogy; that is, *in order to understand a given social phenomenon, we must understand how it contributes to the functioning of society as a whole.* Just as with the human body, one cannot understand the spleen unless one understands how it *functions* for the body as a whole. If we do not understand what the liver does for body, we do not understand the liver.

In *The Rules of the Sociological Method*[1] (1895), Durkheim applied this logic to crime. He noted that since crime occurs in all societies throughout the world and throughout history, it cannot be seen as pathological, or as a sign that there is something wrong with a society. Since crime is universal, it must contribute to the well-being of society. He argued that *crime contributes to the essential function of social cohesion.* Without social cohesion, there would be no such thing as society; we would simply be a number of isolated individuals with nothing in common; but crime brings us together in our mutual abhorrence of the criminal and his crime. Still today, there are few things that we have more in common with our neighbors than our fear and hatred of crime and criminals. *Crime unites us by providing us with a common enemy.*

Durkheim argued that there can be no society without crime; or, as he put it, there cannot be a "society of saints." Here he employed the concept of the "collective conscience," or the lowest common moral denominator in a society. Accordingly, to have a society without murder, the collective conscience would have to be so strong that no one would even consider committing murder. In such a strongly moral society, robbery would be considered as abhorrent as we consider murder. To have a society without robbery, the collective conscience would have to be so strong that no one would even consider committing robbery. In such a strongly moral society, pickpocketing would be considered as abhorrent as we consider murder. To have a society without pickpocketing, the collective conscience would have to be so strong that no one would even consider picking pockets. In such a strongly moral society, jaywalking would be considered as abhorrent as we consider murder and would warrant severe punishment.

Even in a society of saints, the slightest infraction would be considered with the gravity of crime and would trigger grave consequences. Thus, to have a society without crime, everybody would have to think and behave exactly the same. Such a society is impossible and undesirable. If it could exist, such a society would be completely stagnant and never change. Therefore, for Durkheim, *crime is the price we pay for the freedom to think and behave differently from our neighbors; and it is the price we pay for progress.* This is not to say the more crime, the better. Indeed Durkheim felt that modern society engendered too much crime. With modernization, he believed, people become more individualistic, less bound by the norms of society, and increased crime rates are the result.

Following Durkheim, many have noted other functions of crime. Most obviously, crime provides for millions of jobs both inside and outside of the criminal justice system, including police officers, district attorneys, defense attorneys, judges, bailiffs, probation officers, parole officers, prison guards, as well as those who build and supply the prisons, those who sell theft insurance, those who design and manufacture guns and security devices; and the list goes on. Less obviously, *functionalists have noted the role organized crime has played in American history in allowing persecuted minorities to move into the mainstream of American society.* [2] Beginning with the Irish in the middle of the 19th century, then the Jews just after the turn of the 20th century, and then the Italians in the 1930s—when each group of immigrants arrived, they were persecuted, with few legitimate opportunities for success available to them. When some Irish immigrants became successful at organized crime, money began to flow through the Irish community and more opportunities became available for law-abiding Irish immigrants. The same can be said for the Jews and the Italians. Thus organized crime functioned, according to Daniel Bell, as "a queer ladder of social mobility."[3] Supplying illegal goods and services still functions as a means of upward mobility for many ethnic groups.

In a classic extension of Durkheim's functionalist analysis of crime, Kai Erikson argues that crime is necessary in maintaining the moral boundaries of the community.[4] For a community to maintain a sense of identity, it must establish boundaries that distinguish between those who are part of the community and those who are outside of it. This gives community members pride in their membership and a reason to follow the norms of the community. Deviance and reactions to deviance are crucial to this process. *A society needs deviance to publicize its moral boundaries.* Thus, for example, in 18th century England, when hundreds of offenses were punishable by death, public hangings were commonplace. People from the towns and countryside would gather around the gallows, cheering and jeering and having a rollicking good time. This was akin to a rally around the flag, uniting people against a common enemy (Durkheim) and publicizing the community's moral boundaries. The message being conveyed to those present: "We are united in our mutual abhorrence; we are proud of being members of this community; and if you were thinking about stealing someone's cow, this is what will happen to you!" *Once punishments—whipping, branding, tar and feathering, stocks, pillories, hangings, etc.—were performed in public to enhance the cohesive, boundary-maintaining effects of crime. Today, punishment takes place behind prison walls, but media coverage makes crime public and functions with the same effects.*

Do we really believe that if we take a deviant (criminal), lock him up in a deviant environment (prison), with a concentrated population of deviants, and leave him there for years, he will come out less deviant? Erikson helps us to understand this paradoxical reaction to crime when he argues that the true purpose of prison is not to protect society, but to ensure a steady supply of deviants to "patrol" our moral boundaries. Thus the high rates of reoffending among the ex-inmate population is not a sign of the system's failure, but of its success.

4

Social Disorganization Theory
1920s-1940s

Functionalist theory (see Chapter 3) views society as a system of interdependent parts and when one part changes, other parts must change as well. From this perspective, *social change can have disruptive effects as the social system struggles to align its various parts with one another. Social disorganization theory, which employs the same logic, emerged from the University of Chicago in the early 20th century to explain how the momentous social changes of the era were contributing to rising crime rates.* The Sociology Department at the University of Chicago played an instrumental role in the development of American criminology and it has hence become known as the **Chicago School of Criminology**.

Today, people throughout the industrialized world have come to expect social change; but the kinds of social changes that were taking place in Chicago in the first decades of the 20th century were far beyond what people of that era had come to expect. Chicago became a world leader in industrial production. Factory jobs, initially, required few skills, little experience, and they paid relatively well. Consequently, people migrated by the millions from rural America and rural Europe to

Chicago and other urban city centers in the United States.

According to social theorists in the Chicago School, the combination of the immense forces of industrialization, immigration, and urbanization produced a condition of social disorganization. Sociologists W.I. Thomas and Florian Znanecki defined **social disorganization** as "*a decrease of the influence of existing social rules of behavior upon individual members of the group.*"[1] Thus, with massive immigration from rural America and rural Europe, traditional rural values and norms were losing their relevance and the emerging urban values and norms were in a state of flux. In such conditions, with the norms losing their hold on large sectors of the society, crime and delinquency should not be an unexpected result.

Thorsten Sellin used the term "**culture conflict**" to describe a variant of social disorganization. He was referring to the multiplied impacts of the clash between rural American values and urban American values, *and* American values versus the values of immigrants coming from other parts of the world, *together with* the fact that many of those immigrants arriving in American city centers were from rural areas overseas. Sellin writes, "How much greater is not the conflict likely to be when Orient and Occident meet, or when the Corsican mountaineer is transplanted to the lower East Side of New York."[2] *Where there exist so many clashes between rural and urban, native and foreign, culture and* *subculture, the laws will not reflect the values of large segments of the population and crime and delinquency will result.*

Perhaps the most famous and influential of the social disorganization theorists were **Clifford Shaw and Henry McKay**. In their often cited research, Shaw and McKay took a map of Chicago and drew a series of concentric zones, with the city's industrial zone, called the "factory zone," at the center of the map, Moving out from the center was the "zone in transition"," then the "working man's zone," the "residential zone," and the "commuter zone." Essentially, as we moved out from the factories, we moved from poor residential neighborhoods nearest the factories to wealthy neighborhoods farthest from the factories. Then Shaw and McKay pinpointed on the map the addresses of all the kids who came through Cook County Juvenile Court during the time frames that they studied. They found that the pinpoints grew denser as they moved toward the factories; that is, they were densest in the zone in transition. They concluded that delinquency is strongly correlated with one's geographic residence.

As the factory zone adds more industry, the zone enlarges its territory and expands outwards into the zone in transition. The landlords in the zone in transition, expecting to sell off their property to industry, allow their properties to deteriorate, and residents in the zone in transition live in substandard tenement housing.

The zone in transition had the highest delinquency rates and the highest poverty rates. This is the neighborhood where poor immigrants seeking jobs first settled down. Once they could afford to move out, they did; hence, this zone consisted of transitional neighborhoods. With people moving in and out, they did not develop relationships with their neighbors and did not look out for each other's kids. The kids fell in with gangs and when they were brought into court, they were almost always brought in with other kids. This suggested that the zone in transition fostered a culture which was supportive of criminal values and behavior. This supported Shaw and McKay's initial belief that it was the environment, or the culture, that explained delinquency rather than the individual's moral deficiencies, race or ethnicity. Shaw and McKay's work came to be known as **cultural transmission theory**. They wrote, *"This means that the traditions of delinquency can be and are transmitted down through successive generations of boys, in much the same way that language and other social forms are transmitted."*[3]

Shaw and McKay also noted that different neighborhoods were dominated by different ethnic minorities at different times, and that delinquency rates remained relatively constant within a given neighborhood "no matter what group—German, Irish, Scandinavian, Polish, Italian—was living there; but rates for each group had gone down as its members gradually moved out toward the suburbs . . ."[4] This finding further bolstered their contention that *it was the geography and the environment which explained delinquency rather than the moral, ethnic or racial qualities of the individual.*

While social disorganization theory was usefully employed to relate crime and social change in the early decades of 20th century America, it may still have its applications today in other parts of the world that are undergoing similar changes. Until very recently most people in the world lived in rural areas. But in recent decades, as poor countries are developing industrial economies, tens of millions of people every year are moving from the countryside into already overcrowded—some would say "disorganized"—cities for a shot at those factory jobs. As their lifestyles are changing so rapidly, and as cities bring into close vicinity the clashing values and norms of different racial, ethnic, and religious groups, the social disorganization theorist sees the potential for rising crime rates in such environments.

To an extent, social disorganization theory foreshadowed the development of **broken windows theory** *which asserts that signs of social disorder act as an inducement to criminal behavior.* James Q. Wilson and George Kelling write,

If a window in a building is broken and is left unrepaired, all the rest of the windows will soon be broken. This is as true in nice neighborhoods as in rundown ones. Window-breaking does not necessarily occur on a large scale because some areas are inhabited by determined window-breakers whereas others are populated by window-lovers; rather, one unrepaired broken window is a signal that no one cares, and so breaking more windows costs nothing. [5]

Broken windows are not the only inducement to crime, but other signs of social disorder—prostitutes, drugs users, porn shops—"communicate" to potential offenders that the police are essentially off-duty and that they can commit crimes with impunity. When broken windows theory influences law enforcement policy, police are used to "clean up the streets" and officers may engage in questionable use of "stop and frisk" methods.

Social disorganization theory, and more generally, functionalist theory, have conservative implications. A conservative is one who likes to "conserve" or hold on to the status quo and, thus, conservatives, as well as functionalists, tend to be leery of social change and see it as the source of numerous social problems. Commentators have also noted that many of the early adherents of social disorganization theory at the University of Chicago originally came from rural, racially and ethnically homogenous areas and their work reflected a small-town, anti-urban bias which may have been accompanied by racial and ethnic prejudices as well.

These objections notwithstanding, social disorganization theory and the methods employed by its proponents had an enormous impact on social scientists' understanding of urban crime for decades to come.

5

Robert Merton

Social Structure and Anomie[1]
1938

Robert Merton's classic article, "Social Structure and Anomie," published in 1938 in the *American Sociological Review*, may well be the most often cited article in the history of criminology, and among those most often cited in the history of sociology as well.[2] To put this article in perspective, it may be useful to review some concepts developed by the 19th century French sociologist Emile Durkheim (see Chapter 3). Durkheim argued that the principal difference between humans and animals is that, in the state of nature, animals' appetites are limited to their physical needs, whereas human desires are unlimited. That is, in the state of nature, humans could never be satisfied. This is why we are social creatures. We need society to put a limit on our desires, our appetites, our goals. Society limits our expectations through the norms. As it is the norms that regulate our goals, our goals will vary from society to society, and they will vary according to our position in the social structure (i.e., our social class).

Regulating our goals is the most important function of society and the norms that limit our goals are the most important norms. These are the norms that anchor us in society. When they lose their relevance, as when they set our goals unrealistically high (for example, during an economic depression) or unrealistically low (during an economic boom) then people lose their anchor and are set adrift in a sea of meaningless. This, according to Durkheim, is a condition called **anomie** and it helps us to understand why suicide rates go up during *both* an economic bust and an economic boom.[3]

Merton's article reflected and diverged from Durkheim's thesis in significant ways. Importantly, while Durkheim saw human desires as being present in the state of nature, Merton argued that our desires are culturally induced, with different cultures setting different goals for their members. Thus, one society might set military heroism as a preeminent goal, another may set honoring one's family, another may set service to God; each society is distinctive in the goals that it sets. The United States, according to Merton, is distinctive in the preeminence it gives to the goal of financial success. Here again, he departed from Durkheim: while Durkheim said that the limits on our goals depend upon our position in the social structure (that is, members of the lower class have lower expectations than members of the upper class), Merton disagreed, arguing that everybody in the United States—regardless of class—wants to get rich. So important is the goal of financial success in the United States that we have even named this goal after our country—*the American Dream*. So important is the emphasis placed on the goal of financial success that it becomes a measure of our success in life.

The American Dream is foisted on all Americans; we are told that it is achievable by all; and this claim is based on the presupposition that there is equal opportunity in the United States. Here is the first problem: there is *not* equal opportunity in the United States. The proof of that is simple and irrefutable. It is much more difficult to get rich if you are born poor than it is to stay rich if you are born rich. The notion that there is equal opportunity is essentially a lie. A related problem is that American institutions are simply not equipped to provide financial success to everybody. Thus, *while all well-socialized Americans are striving for financial success, tens of millions are being set up for failure—especially those in the lower rungs of the social hierarchy—because there is not equal opportunity and because society's institutions are not equipped to provide wealth for all.*

Not only do cultures specify the goals for which their members are to aspire, but they also specify the means by which they are to achieve them. In the United States, we are supposed to aspire for the goal of financial success by means of hard work and following the rules. *Another problem identified by Merton is that American society places such enormous emphasis on the goal of financial success that the emphasis placed on the legitimate means of achieving success pales in comparison.* Thus, it is not how you play the game, but whether you win or lose.

Merton and Durkheim converge on the point of anomie. The norms which place so much emphasis on the goal of financial success and that tell us that it is achievable by all through hard work and following the rules are misaligned with reality. These norms are irrelevant to millions of Americans, especially those from the lower class who have worked hard and followed the rules and they are still poor. Or, perhaps more to the point, they have seen their parents and grandparents who have worked hard all of their lives and who are still living in poverty. For them, the norms have lost their meaning. And *since these norms that set our goals are the most important of norms, when they lose their meaning, other norms start to lose their meaning as well, such as it is wrong to lie, cheat, and steal. The result is anomie, or, in Merton's words, "normlessness."*

In such a situation as that outlined by Merton, there are several possible "modes of adaptation." He depicted them graphically as seen in Table 5.1 Examining this table, we see the **conformist** is an individual who accepts the goal of financial success and accepts the means of hard work and following the rules. This is what all well-socialized Americans are supposed to do. The **innovator** accepts the goal of financial success, but rejects the means and attempts to achieve success by breaking the rules. This mode of adaptation is the one of most interest to criminologists; it includes drug dealing, robbery, embezzlement and just about every criminal activity oriented toward financial gain. The **ritualist** is one who has given up on the goal of financial success, but still goes through the motions and plays by the rules. The **retreatist** gives up on both the goals and the means and "withdraws" from the game prescribed by the norms. This category might include hardcore homeless alcoholics and drug addicts. And the **rebel** rejects the goal of financial success and the means of following the

Modes of Adaptation	Cultural Goals	Institutional Means
Conformity	+	+
Innovation	+	–
Ritualism	–	+
Retreatism	–	–
Rebellion	±	±

Table 5.1: Merton's "Modes of Adaptation"

rules and replaces them both with his or her own goals and means. This might include someone who joins a monastery or a religious cult, or perhaps even a terrorist.

The popularity and longevity of Merton's theory lies in the fact that it makes the connection between crime and poverty in a specifically American context. While his theory is specific to American society, it has implications for the understanding of crime in general. If there is a connection between crime and poverty, as has been postulated for centuries, why does the United States, the wealthiest country in the world, have some of the highest crime rates in the industrialized world? Merton's theory suggests that there are two interrelated answers to this question. First, while other countries may have higher rates of poverty, the correlation between crime and poverty is not as strong in those societies because the emphasis on financial success and the belief in equal opportunity are not as strong; therefore, it may well be that the frustration engendered by poverty is not as keen in those countries as it is in the United States.

Merton's theory would also suggest that the higher rates of crime in the United States has to do not just with the misalignment between culturally prescribed goals and the institutional means of achieving those goals, but to the particular configuration of that misalignment. If we lived in a society where the preeminent goal prescribed for us all was to honor our family, this is a goal that could theoretically be achieved by us and all of our fellow citizens; and, if we found our path to be blocked for some reason, breaking the law is not likely to help us bring honor to our family; it would quite likely do the opposite and bring them shame. Instead, Americans live in a society where the preeminent goal is financial success; millions of

Americans are set up to fail in achieving that goal if they restrict themselves to legitimate means; but they may be able to achieve that goal through the commission of crime. In other words, the particular configuration of the misalignment between goals and means in the United States is such that achievement of the culturally prescribed goal can be brought about by the commission of crime. If the goal were different, that would not likely be the case.

6

Edwin Sutherland

Differential Association[1]
White Collar Crime
1939, 1940

There are few people as influential in the history of
American criminology as Edwin Sutherland. His theory of
differential association is one of the most recognizable
theories in 2oth century criminology. But possibly more
importantly, his influence extends from the fact that his
book, *Principles of Criminology*, first published in 1924,
was one of the best-selling textbooks in the field for
many decades, with the eleventh edition published in
1992. (Sutherland died in 1950 and the continuation of
his book depended upon coauthor Donald Cressey and
later, David Luckenbill.) Through the remarkable
longevity of his textbook, Sutherland played a major role
in establishing criminology as a subdiscipline of sociology
throughout most of the 20th century and he influenced
the range of subjects that would be included in the
"standard" undergraduate criminology course. His
theory of differential association made its first
appearance in the 1939 edition of his textbook.

For Sutherland, criminal behavior is normal. By that, he meant *that criminal behavior is learned the same way that all behavior is learned—through our social interactions, or "associations", with others in our environment.* Hailing from the University of Chicago, Sutherland was influenced by social disorganization theory (see Chapter 4); but he took issue with the term. High crime areas are not "disorganized;" in fact, they are often highly organized, as they must be when they include illegal drug networks, gambling operations, prostitution rings, extortion rackets, and the like. So instead of characterizing high crime areas as disorganized, he said they were organized differently, or "differentially" organized. *The way one's environment— or area, or neighborhood—is organized will determine the nature and quality of his or her associations; and those associations will determine what he or she learns.* Sutherland's theory is depicted in Figure 6.1.

According to Sutherland, *people who live in high crime areas are likely to associate with others who have little respect for the law and, from them, they are likely to learn "techniques of committing the crime" and "definitions" which predispose them to criminal behavior.* "A person becomes delinquent," he writes, "because of an excess of definitions favorable to violation of law over definitions unfavorable to violation of law."[2] To be more specific, he writes,

In some societies an individual is surrounded by persons who invariably define legal codes as rules to be observed, while in others he is surrounded by persons whose definitions are favorable to the violation of legal codes. In our American society these definitions are almost always mixed, with the consequence that we have a culture conflict in relation to the legal codes.[3]

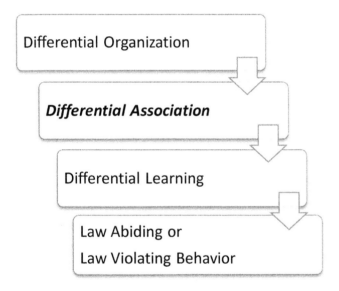

Figure 6.1: Sutherland's Theory of Differential Association

On its face, differential association boils down to what mothers have been telling their children for thousands of years: "hang around with bums and you'll become a bum." This analogy is, of course, an oversimplification because by the word "association," Sutherland was referring to the process of communication and the content of that communication, and whether or not that content favors violation of the law. Thus, one does not have to hang out with criminals to acquire criminal definitions; he or she could pick up criminal definitions from contacts with non-criminals as well.

A problem we encounter thus far might be called the problem of "differential response." Namely, some people hang around with criminals and do *not* become criminals; while some people who have not hung around with criminals *do* become criminals. But again, Sutherland was not actually referring to the criminal status of those we interact with, but to the content of our communications with them. To further address the problem of differential response, *Sutherland delineated several dimensions or "modalities" of association: frequency, duration, priority, and intensity.* "Frequency" and "duration," he writes, are dimensions of association that "are obvious and need no explanation." By "priority," he was referring to the stage in life when one begins his or her criminal associations; and by "intensity," he referred to the "emotional reactions related to the associations."[4]

While differential association was enormously influential in 20th century American criminology, the theory has been impervious to empirical testing. Namely, it is impossible to measure the content of a lifetime of communications for just one individual, let alone a sample or class of individuals (i.e., criminals). Further, it would be very difficult to measure the modalities of association and to determine how they should be weighted. Sutherland, himself, writes,

In the precise description of the criminal behavior of a person these modalities would be stated in quantitative form and a mathematical ratio be reached. A formula in this sense has not been developed, and the development of such a formula would be extremely difficult.[5]

Despite the problem of empirical verification, there are a number of factors that explain the popularity of differential association. Probably the most important factor has already been mentioned above and that is that Sutherland wrote the textbook that became the standard in American criminology and he was able to promote the theory through his book. Further, the theory's appeal relates to the fact that it is a theory about the effects of bad parental and bad peer influence on bad behavior, and such effects have always been presumed by professionals and laymen alike. Sutherland articulated that influence in the language of sociology and gave it academic credibility. And lastly, the logic of differential association was employed or assumed in a number of important criminological theories that were to follow Sutherland, thus assuring the longevity of his theory.

Before leaving our discussion of Sutherland, another important contribution of his to criminology is worthy of note. He introduced the concept of "white collar crime" in his presidential address to the American Sociological Society in 1940. (According to one biographical sketch, it "was one of the few such addresses that received front-page publicity in the daily newspapers."[6]) *He defined white collar crime as "crime committed by a person of respectability and high social status in the course of his occupation."*[7] His recognition of white collar crime became a milestone in the history of criminology. Before this recognition, criminologists concerned themselves almost exclusively with crimes committed by the poor and with the "underworld" of crime. Sutherland paved the way for the study of crimes committed by corporations and by the elite and he made way for the study of the relationship between crime and work.

7

Albert Cohen

Delinquent Subcultures[1]
1955

Albert Cohen was one among several prominent sociologists in the 1950s and early '60s who focused their attention on the formation and activities of lower and working class male gang delinquents. Cohen characterizes the behavior of these gangs as being non-utilitarian, malicious, and negativistic. By *non-utilitarian*, he meant that their delinquent activities do not seem oriented toward a purpose. When they steal, for example, they usually are not stealing anything that will be of use to them; instead they seem to steal at random, take things they do not need, and often destroy those things. By *malicious*, he meant that they seem to take pride in being "just plain mean." And by *negativistic*, Cohen meant that these juvenile gangs seem to take the dominant middle class norms, turn them upside down, and do the opposite of what is expected of them. Cohen writes,

> The same spirit is evident in playing hookey and in misbehavior in school. The teacher and her rules are not merely something onerous to be evaded. They

are to be *flouted*. There is an element of active spite and malice, contempt and ridicule, challenge and defiance, exquisitely symbolized, in an incident described by writer Henry D. McKay, of defecating on the teacher's desk. . . . The delinquent's conduct is right by the standards of his subculture, precisely *because* it is wrong by the norms of the larger culture. "Malicious" and "negativistic" are foreign to the delinquent's vocabulary but he will often assure us, sometimes ruefully, sometimes with a touch of glee or even pride, the he is "just plain mean."[2]

Much of Cohen's theory goes on to explain why the lower class male gang delinquent behaves as he described above.

According to Cohen, everybody seeks status. That is, we all want recognition; we all want to be held in the esteem of others because our self-esteem depends upon the esteem of others. In short, we all need to feel good about ourselves. Sociologists distinguish between ascribed status and achieved status. *Ascribed status* is essentially status that we are born with, whereas *achieved status* is status that we achieve, that is the result of our actions. *Kids born into lower and working class families are born with little or no ascribed status, so any chance they have of finding the esteem of others will have to be derived from achievement.* The environment in which most kids achieve legitimate status is in the school system. Unfortunately, these kids are forced to compete for status against middle class kids in a middle class school system, with middle class administrators and middle class teachers who have middle class values and middle class prejudices. In other words, *they are born with little or no status and the deck is stacked against them when it comes to achieving status. The normal avenues for feeling good about themselves are blocked.*

Kids in this situation can adapt in one of several ways. Some will buckle down on their school work, intent on going to college. To succeed, they will have to distance themselves from the influence of their lower or working class peers, and sometimes from their own parents and families who may place little value on academics. Other kids will give up and hang out on street corners with kids like themselves.

Another mode of adaptation involves the gang. *Often, these kids will gravitate toward one another and reward each other status, based on their ability to offend the dominant middle class culture which has blocked other avenues to status attainment.* They revel in their defiance of the middle class and its norms and values. Their defiance manifests itself in delinquent behavior. So why do their crimes appear non-utilitarian? Why are their behaviors so malicious and negativistic? Indeed, their crimes *are* utilitarian when one understands that their goal is to achieve status within their gang. And their behaviors are malicious and negativistic because these are the attributes which will win them status among their peers. The standards of the gang evolved as a reaction to the deprivation of status through legitimate means in the broader society. So why a drive-by shooting? Street cred.

8

Gresham Sykes

Techniques of Neutralization[1]
The Society of Captives[2]
1957, 1958

Gresham Sykes is renowned for two seminal works in criminology, both published within a year of each other. One was a book, derived from his Ph.D. dissertation, entitled *The Society of Captives: A Study of a Maximum Security Prison*. The other was an article, coauthored with **David Matza** and published in the *American Sociological Review*, entitled "Techniques of Neutralization." This latter work was published first and is still republished often and the theory it contains has been applied to a wide range of behaviors. It will be discussed first.

Sykes and Matza's article "Techniques of Neutralization" has been and continues to be a staple in any criminological education. The authors begin the article by taking issue with some of their contemporaries and asserting that the value sets of juvenile delinquents are much the same as those of the rest of us. Popular idols—movie stars and famous athletes—represent our values, and delinquents uphold the same idols as other kids their age. Furthermore, juvenile delinquents draw

48

strong lines between those people who can and cannot be victimized; and sometimes, juveniles may feel guilty for their crimes. In other words, juvenile delinquents are aware of the wrongfulness of their acts. Having made this argument, *Sykes and Matza ask the very important question, Why do people violate the rules in which they believe? The answer lies in the fact that the rules are not stated as absolutes.* In fact, one of the first rules that we learn is that there are exceptions to every rule. We learn, for example, that it is wrong to kill; but it is alright to kill in war. We learn that it is wrong to lie; but a "little white lie" to preserve a friend's self-esteem is alright. *The problem for juvenile delinquents is that they learn to recognize exceptions to the rules that are not recognized by the law.* Sykes and Matza call these exceptions that are recognized by juvenile delinquents "techniques of neutralization"—that is, techniques by which juveniles neutralize the wrongfulness of their acts—and they identify five such techniques.

The first technique is **denial of responsibility**. In this case, the juvenile denies responsibility for his actions, instead claiming, for example, that it was an accident, or blaming his actions on peer pressure or unloving parents. Here, the juvenile sees him or herself as "more acted upon than acting." The second technique Sykes and Matza identify is **denial of injury**. Here, the juvenile may explain auto theft as "just borrowing" the car; or, they may see vandalism or bullying as "just a prank." The next technique is **denial of the victim**. In this case, the juvenile, for example, may blame an assault on the victim, saying "they should know better than to come into our neighborhood." Here, they see the victim as "asking for it." The next technique is **condemnation of the condemners**. With this technique, the juvenile diverts the attention away from the wrongfulness of his or her behavior and onto that of their accusers. In this case, they see their behaviors as no worse than those of other kids, but "the teacher is always picking on me," or the "the cop is a racist." The last technique is **appeal to higher loyalties**. Examples of this technique might include: "he beat up on one of my buds," or "he called my sister a 'slut'." In this case, the juvenile does not deny the wrongfulness of his or her actions, but other loyalties take precedence.

According to the theory, these techniques should not be viewed as "mere" excuses or rationalizations. The juvenile actually believes in the logic of these techniques; such beliefs are present *before* the delinquent behavior takes place, and they pave the way for the delinquency. We all need to believe that we are right and that we are good people. It is the belief in these techniques that enables the juvenile to commit acts of delinquency and still feel good about him- or herself.

The influence of neutralization theory has extended far beyond the literature in juvenile delinquency. It has been used to explain such behaviors as deer poaching, soliciting prostitutes, entering children into beauty pageants, and many other behaviors, both legal and illegal.

The other work for which Sykes is well-renowned is *The Society of Captives*, a brief book describing and explaining the prison culture. Several of its chapters became classics in their own right. Among criminologists, the most recognizable concept from the book is the "pains of imprisonment."

The culture of maximum security inmates is well known to be an extremely volatile and violent one, populated by exceedingly unsavory characters. Before Sykes, the popular explanation for these qualities of the prison culture was known as the *importation model*. This common-sense model explained that society has imported its most volatile, violent and unsavory members and concentrated them in one place, the prison, and therefore, it should come as no surprise that the prison culture takes on those same qualities. Sykes proposed, instead, the *adaptation model* of the prison culture, arguing that it is the way it is as a consequence of prisoners adapting to the five pains of imprisonment.

The first pain of imprisonment is the **deprivation of liberty**. The very act of incarceration signifies a moral rejection by the larger society and sends a message to the offender that he is so despised that he is not worthy of living among us. This represents an assault on the offender's self-worth and requires that he learn to "reject his rejectors"—that is, judge society as being unworthy of judging him—in order to live with himself. The second pain of imprisonment is the **deprivation of material goods**. The prisoner is severely limited in terms of the objects that he can have in his possession. This represents an assault on the prisoner's selfhood, especially in American society, where people identify themselves so much in terms of what they own. The third pain of imprisonment is the **deprivation of heterosexual relationships**. This is a further threat to the self in that we identify ourselves so much in terms of our sex and sexuality. The next pain of imprisonment is the **deprivation of autonomy**. The prisoner is subjected to a multitude of often trivial, seemingly capricious, rules of the prison regime. If the prisoner asks why he is not allowed to do this and such, a guard is likely to respond, "because that's the rule," or "because I said so." This is much the way their parents would have responded, thus reducing the prisoner to the status of a child, and threatening his selfhood. The last pain of imprisonment is the **deprivation of security**. It is said that the worse part of living in prison is that you have to live with other prisoners. Besides the physical threat, this is also a threat to the prisoner's selfhood because he knows that no matter where he is in the pecking order, he may have to prove *himself on* any day at any time.

To sum up Sykes's thesis, imprisonment represents an all-out assault of the prisoner's selfhood and the ways in which prisoners have to respond or "adapt" to this assault contribute to the violent nature of the prison culture and are not conducive to the prisoner's rehabilitation. With Sykes's thesis in mind, it is not necessary to reject the importation model, but an understanding of the prison culture is far from complete without an understanding of this adaptation process.

In 2001, more than forty years after the publication of *The Society of Captives* author Michael Reisig surveyed a number of well-published scholars in criminology to determine the most influential books written in prison studies. *The Society of Captives* was ranked number 1.[3]

9

Labeling Theory

1950s, '60s and '70s

Labeling theory has quite an extensive theoretical pedigree. In large part, it is a specific application of a theoretical approach, called **symbolic interactionism**, to crime and deviance. In order to grasp the principles of labeling theory, it will be helpful to understand the concept of **the self** as it was developed by early symbolic interactionists.

According to Charles Horton Cooley, the self is made up of three components: 1) the imagination of our appearance to others, 2) the imagination of their judgment of our appearance, and 3) pride or shame.[1] In other words, our perception of our self is made up of our perceptions of other peoples' perceptions of us. (It is not made up of their actual perceptions because we cannot get into their heads and know exactly what they are thinking.) That is, if you think you are cool, it is because you think other people think you are cool; if you think you are fat, it is because you think other people think you are fat. In which case, "cool" or "fat" become part of your self. Another leading figure—actually *the* leading figure—in the development of symbolic interactionism was George Herbert Mead. *For Mead, people do not respond to reality, they, instead, respond to their perceptions of reality and those perceptions are learned through social interaction.*[2] We all perceive, or interpret, reality differently because no two people have been exposed to the exact same series of human interactions. The interpretations that are most important in understanding human behavior are our **definition of the self** and our **definition of the situation**

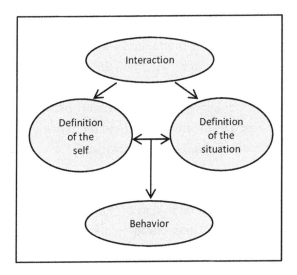

Figure 9.1: The Symbolic Interactionist Model

which, again, are both the products of social interaction. Figure 9.1 summarizes the essence of symbolic interactionism.

We will return to symbolic interactionism in a moment; but first we will discuss the distinction made by Edwin Lemert between primary and secondary deviance.[3] Primary deviance happens for any number of reasons that are of little or no concern to the labeling theorist; instead, the labeling theorist is concerned with secondary deviance. *Secondary deviance is deviance that results from having been labeled deviant; that is, a deviant label tends to act as a self-fulfilling prophecy.* There are a number of reasons that explain why this is the case. When someone is labeled "deviant," he or she is being stigmatized, identified as different, singled out. The quality of their interactions with others is altered. The opportunity for "normal" interactions becomes more limited. Making the case that it is normal for teenagers to engage in mischievous behavior, Frank Tannenbaum noted how only some teens are singled out and their world changed in the process:

> There is a gradual shift from the definition of specific acts as evil to a definition of the individual as evil, so that all of his acts come to be looked upon with suspicion. In the process of identification his companions, hang-outs, play, speech, income, all his conduct, the personality itself, become objects of scrutiny and question.[4]

According to symbolic interactionism, our behavior is, in significant measure, a product of our definition of self, and our definition of self is derived from social interaction. Thus, *if people act toward us as though we are deviant, a deviant identity will be incorporated into our definition of self. Rejected by "normal" members of the community, someone so labeled will likely gravitate toward others who have been so labeled.* The teenager, for example, who has been labeled delinquent, says Tannenbaum, comes slowly to recognize "that the definition of him as a human being is different from that of other boys in his neighborhood, his school, street, community. This recognition on his part becomes a process of self-identification and integration with the group which shares his activities."[5]

We should note that labeling is a process, and to state that a deviant label is a self-fulfilling prophecy is an over-simplification. Instead, it is more accurate to say that someone who has been *successfully* labeled deviant is likely to engage in secondary deviance.

Another element of labeling theory is that its focus is often more upon the labelers (the audience) and less upon the criminal and his or her behavior. Prior to the advent of labeling theory, the works of criminologists tended to assume that there was something inherent in the criminal that made him or her bad, or something inherent in the criminal activity that made it bad. Criminologists saw themselves as problem solvers and crime, they assumed, was inherently problematic. However, noting that the definitions of crime vary from time to time and place to place, in the 1950s and 1960s sociologists began to question the meaning of the word "crime." Since it is difficult to identify any behaviors that are defined as crime in all cultures throughout history, it follows that there is nothing inherent in crime that makes it a "crime." Instead, to understand crime, we must examine the society, the culture, the laws, and the labelers.

On these points, labeling theory and conflict theory often converge. Remember that conflict theory (see Chapter 2) focuses on unequal power relations and on how different groups use their power to further their own interests. People and groups with power have the ability to affix deviant labels on people and groups without power and they do so to further their own interests. With this in mind, an examination of history reveals that drug legislation in the United States, for example, has had less to do with the control of inherently dangerous drugs than it has had to do with the control of various minority groups who have been perceived by those in power to be a threat. Thus, writes David Musto,

> The most passionate support for legal prohibition of narcotics has been associated with fear of a given drug's effect on a specific minority. Certain drugs were dreaded because they seemed to undermine essential social restrictions which kept these groups under control: cocaine was supposed to enable blacks to withstand bullets which would kill normal persons and to stimulate sexual assault. Fear that smoking opium facilitated sexual contact between Chinese

and white Americans was also a factor in its total prohibition. Chicanos in the Southwest were believed to be incited to violence by smoking marijuana. Heroin was linked in the 1920s with a turbulent age group: adolescents in reckless and promiscuous urban gangs. Alcohol was associated with immigrants crowding into large and corrupt cities. In each instance, use of a particular drug was attributed to an identifiable and threatening minority group.[6]

In other words, *minority group members are more likely to be labeled as drug offenders not necessarily because they use more drugs, nor because they represent a greater threat to society than non-minority group members, but because of their minority group status.*

It is because of such analyses that labeling theory struck a chord and had a prominent influence in criminology and criminal justice during the civil rights movement in the 1950s and '60s, and partly into the 1970s. Its influence was clearly on the downswing in the 1980s, due in part, to a conservative backlash to the social justice reforms of the civil rights era.

10

Joseph Gusfield

Status Politics[1]
1963

Joseph Gusfield made a name for himself primarily in the field of sociology and his name is not often referenced in criminology textbooks today. However, his work on the study of social movements has many implications for crime and criminology. Gusfield's seminal work, *Symbolic Crusade: Status Politics and the American Temperance Movement*, was published in 1963. In it he examines the forces that gave rise to the criminalization of alcohol consumption during Prohibition in the United States in the early part of the 20th century. This was a time when there was massive immigration into the United States. Prior to this wave of immigration, the United States was largely rural; and white Protestants were comfortably in control of political, cultural and economic arrangements in the country. But the new wave of immigrants in the late 19th and early 20th century was composed largely of non-Protestants— Catholics from Ireland and Italy, and Jews from Eastern Europe—taking up residence in bustling urban centers. The Protestant establishment felt their control and their lifestyles were being threatened by this influx of immigrants.

With regard to lifestyle, one important difference between the established Protestants and the new immigrants revolved around the role of alcohol. The Temperance Movement was already well underway in the United States before the Catholics and Jews were arriving *en masse*, and this movement had been embraced by Protestant clergy and by millions of their followers. Temperance became very much a religious concern. Alcohol consumption was increasingly viewed as a sinful and corrupting influence in American society. Then came the new immigrants, among whom alcohol consumption had been integrated into their cultures, and even into their religious ceremonies. *Alcohol consumption came to symbolize the differences between Protestants and the newly arriving immigrants, and the Temperance Movement took on a new urgency among Protestants.* This urgency culminated in the passage of the 18th Amendment, which banned alcohol and which took effect in 1919.

Organized crime flourished during Prohibition because of the enormous profits that could be made in providing the public with this newly illicit substance. With organized crime came massive corruption among public officials and a great deal of violence in America's urban centers as crime syndicates maneuvered to establish their territories. Millions of Americans flaunted the law and became criminals, as they continued to consume alcohol. Today, Prohibition is regarded by most Americans to have been a massive failure. But, *according to Gusfield, despite the fact that Prohibition caused so many social problems and had only a modest effect in curbing people's alcohol consumption, it still represented a* **symbolic victory** *for the Protestants.* The passage of Prohibition was a demonstration of the power that the Protestant establishment still wielded over American society. They had control of the law and they were able to criminalize the behavior of millions of recent immigrants.

Gusfield describes the activities leading up to the passage of the 18th amendment as an exercise in **status politics***, with different interest groups competing with one another to assert the moral superiority of their norms and values through the enactment of law.* Today, a controversial law in France, for example, bans the wearing of the *burqa* and the *niqab*, the traditional attire worn by Muslim women. Such legislation degrades the moral authority of the Muslim religion, damages the status of Muslims in the French population, and criminalizes their religious traditions.

Legislation banning alcohol and the burqa are examples of status politics involving different religions. Today, such conflicts are often not so much between different religions as they are between religious conservatives and secular liberals. The ever-changing legislation regarding abortion in the United States pits both Catholic and Protestant devotees against secular liberals. Much the same can be said about the controversy over same-sex marriage and perhaps even the legalization of marijuana. In any case, the "losing" side in each battle in the "culture wars" has the status of its values officially degraded by the legislature, and behaviors they regard as "rights" may well be criminalized.

11

Travis Hirschi

Control Theory[1]
1969

Most criminological theories start with the question, "Why did he or she commit the crime?" Travis Hirschi, instead, started with the question, "Why doesn't everybody commit the crime?" Criminal behavior, after all, is not difficult to understand. Fred saw something in the store he wanted, but he did not have the money to pay for it, so he stealthily put it into his pocket and left the store. Such behavior, according to Hirschi, is not difficult to understand. It is more difficult to understand why everybody does not put unpurchased merchandise into their pockets. Other criminological theories may ask the question, "What is present in the criminal's environment or psyche that makes him or her different from non-criminals?" Hirschi, instead, addresses the problem in terms of "What is absent?" The answer, in a word, is "controls." These controls take the form of bonds between the individual and society. *The criminal is a person for whom the bonds between him- or herself and society are weaker than normal.*

Hirschi's control theory is not the first of its kind. Freudian theory, as it is applied to criminal behavior, for example, represents a form of control theory. For Freud, the personality is made up of three components: the **id**, the **ego**, and the **superego**. The id constitutes one's biological or natural drives; the ego is the part of the self that accommodates to the realities of society to achieve some satisfaction of the id; and the superego is the conscience, or the guilt we feel when we satisfy our id in socially inappropriate ways. Thus, the two-year-old child reaching for cookies in spite of her Mommy's admonishments is expressing her id. The four-year-old child who waits for Mommy to leave the room to sneak a cookie is expressing her ego. And the six-year-old child who waits for Mommy to leave the room, hesitates, feels guilty, and withdraws her hand without a cookie is expressing her superego. For Freud, the individual's personality consists of the balance between these three components of the self, with the ego and the superego acting as social controls. The absence of a properly developed ego or superego make way for a poorly controlled id which is likely to express itself in amoral or criminal behavior.

Freud's theory of the personality concerns the absence of psychological controls. Hirschi's theory concerns the absence of *sociological* controls. *Hirschi identified four types of bonds between the individual and society which serve as social controls: attachment, commitment, involvement, and belief.* **Attachment** *refers* *to the extent to which one is concerned about the desires and feelings of others.* For example, a person may refrain from criminal behavior because he worries that being arrested would bring shame to his loved ones. (This would be sociological counterpart to Freud's superego, referring, that is, to the guilt an individual feels at the prospect of shaming his loved ones.) **Commitment** *refers to one's investment in conventional society that could be lost by engaging in criminal activity.* If arrested, the individual could lose her job, her house, her kids. (This is the sociological counterpart to Freud's ego as the individual negotiates the rules of society and engages in a cost/benefit analysis of what she has to gain by criminal behavior versus what she has to lose.) **Involvement** *refers to the extent to which one is engaged in conventional society.* Hirschi writes,

> The person involved in conventional activities is tied to appointments, deadlines, working hours, plans, and the like, so the opportunity to commit deviant acts rarely arises. To the extent that he is engaged in conventional activities, he cannot even think about deviant acts, let alone act out his inclinations.[2]

Lastly, **belief** *refers to the extent to which an individual subscribes to conventional notions of right and wrong.* When this bond between the individual and society is weak, the individual does not have "an attitude of respect toward the rules of society . . . and feels no moral obligation to conform regardless of personal advantage."[3]

As there is significant overlap between the different types of bonds between the individual and society that were identified by Hirschi, it is difficult to put his theory to the test. His theory most likely remains a classic in American criminology, though, because it so well explains why crime rates are so much higher in the United States than in so many other countries. The contrast is particularly striking, for example, when we compare American crime rates to those of Japan. Control theory suggests that crime rates are so high in the United States because of the premium its culture places on individualism; whereas Japanese crime rates are so low because of the value it places on collectivism.

Collectivist societies, such as Japan, often place a high value on honoring one's parents (attachment); in such societies, people's identity is strongly tied to their work or their workplace (commitment); In Japan, children often attend juku ("cram schools") after school or on weekends in preparation for their college entrance exams (involvement). Together, factors such as these are likely to strengthen the Japanese adherence to a common value system (belief).

By contrast, "individualism," by its very nature, suggests that the bonds between the individual and society are weak. Arguably, Americans might care less about shaming their parents than the Japanese; they have less to lose in terms of their group commitments;

and, spending more time alone or at home, they are less involved in communal activities. According to control theory, the lack of such inhibitions promotes higher crime rates in the United States.

12

Stanley Cohen

Moral Panics[1]
1972

Crime can be a fearful phenomenon and it has captivated the public imagination for centuries, if not millennia. Kings, presidents, senators, congressmen, police chiefs and mayors have raised the specter of crime to rally support behind them. From the broadsides of early 18th century, to the earliest days of the newspaper, to the modern crime novel, publishers have long known that crime "sells." With political leaders, bureaucrats and the media capitalizing on crime, it is not surprising that crime "waves" get blown out of proportion and people get the impression that the threat of crime is far greater than the reality it presents. While criminologists have long recognized this phenomenon, it was British sociologist Stanley Cohen who analyzed it systematically and popularized its identification as a "moral panic."[2]

In his book, *Folk Devils and Moral Panics*, Cohen analyzed an incident occurring in the beach resort town of Clacton on a holiday in 1964. Two groups of youths—later to be known as the Mods and the Rockers—bored because it was too cold to enjoy the beach that day, engaged in acts of mischief. Cohen describes their behavior, "Those on bikes and scooters roared up and down, windows were broken, beach huts were wrecked and one boy fired a starting pistol in the air."[3] The incident made national headlines, depicting it as though it were an invasion of violent biker gangs marauding the seaside. "Words and phrases such as 'riot,' 'orgy of destruction,' 'battle,' 'attack,' 'siege,' 'beat up the town,' and 'screaming mob'"[4] were deployed in the reporting of the incident. Politicians decried the state of England's youth, creating the impression that this was the first of many such incidents to come. Police throughout the country were put on high alert. Indeed, such an incident did follow in Whitsun and, even though it was *less* disruptive than the one in Clacton, it was also characterized by the media with the same hyperbole as the incident in Clacton. One media outlet characterized the participants in Whitsun as "long-haired youngsters with knives indulging in an orgy of hooliganism."[56]

Cohen pointed out that all news agencies have to be selective in the information that they distribute—because all of the information in the world simply cannot be distributed through the news—and *certain subjects are far more likely to make it through the news filter into the public imagination. Crime and deviance figure prominently among those subjects.* Cohen writes,

It is not that instruction manuals exist telling newsmen that certain subjects (drugs, sex, violence)

will appeal to the public or that certain groups (youth, immigrants) should be continually exposed to scrutiny. Rather, there are built-in factors, ranging from the individual newsman's intuitive hunch about what constitutes a "good story," through precepts such as "give the public what it wants" to structured ideological biases, which predispose the media to make a certain event into news.[7]

Such news reportage sensitizes the public, and other issues come to be seen as related to the original disturbance and symbolic of deeper problems in the society. The deeper problem in Cohen's analysis was the popular perception that England's younger generation was undisciplined and out of control. Thus, with the Clacton incident having resonated so well among the media, politicians, and the public, other issues that might be only slightly related to the theme of undisciplined youth suddenly became newsworthy, further fueling the moral panic. Kenneth Thompson writes,

As a result of sensitization, incidents that might have been written off as "horseplay" or a "dance hall brawl" were interpreted as being part of the Mods and Rockers phenomenon. Public nervousness increased and there was pressure for more police vigilance and stronger action from the forces of law and order. The police then reacted by stepping up patrols and increasing their interventions in potential trouble spots—seaside towns, dance halls, fairs and other public events. Court proceedings reflected the sensitization.[8]

The moral panics literature suggests that *the public is more susceptible to being misled by alarmist reports of crime during periods of momentous social change. Such change creates uncertainty and anxiety, and the issue which is the focus of the moral panic comes to symbolize the threat of social change.* Jeffrey Victor calls the moral panic a "collective nightmare,"[9] just as nightmares purportedly are a symbolic representation of anxieties we may have experienced during the day. The moral panic over the Mods and the Rockers had to do with the immense social changes taking place in post-war Britain. Life had been hard for the British during the Depression and got even harder during World War II. By 1964, conditions had improved enormously and the older generation was sensing that the youth were getting by too easily; they were not learning the lessons that come from hardship; they were spoiled and had no moral compass. A nerve had been exposed, and the incident at Clacton tapped into these fears. Such are the makings of a moral panic.

Another classic moral panic took place in the United States in the 1980s. This had to do with the panic over "satanic ritual abuse" alleged to be taking place in day care centers around the country. It began with hundreds of allegations of sexual assault at the McMartin Preschool in California in 1983. These led to a trial lasting more than two years, and costing more than any trial in the U.S. history up to that point. There were no convictions. But *the "cultural response to the McMartin case," writes Mary deYoung,*

> *had all of the characteristics of what sociologists call a moral panic: it was **widespread, volatile, hostile, and overreactive**. . .* From Texas to Tennessee, New Jersey to North Carolina, Maine to Michigan, hundreds of local day care centers were investigated for satanic ritual abuse and scores of day care providers, as many males as females, were arrested and put on trial. From the witness stand, their accusers, the three- and four-year-old children once entrusted to their care, accused them of sexual abuse during satanic ceremonies that included such ghastly practices as blood-drinking, cannibalism, and human sacrifices. Despite the absence of evidence corroborating the children's accounts, many of the day care providers were convicted, and to the cheers and jeers of their deeply divided communities, were sentenced to what often were draconian prison terms.[10]

deYoung's description of the children's allegations in the 1980s may strike the reader as similar to the notorious witch trials in Salem, Massachusetts in the early 17th century; and indeed, those historic events had all of the qualities that mark a moral panic.

According to deYoung, the social change that made the public susceptible to misleading information in the 1980s was the massive movement of women into the workplace. Almost all of a sudden, millions of parents began leaving their young children in the care of virtual strangers. This created anxiety, exposing a nerve, and the McMartin case "proved" parents' worst fears. They became sensitized to the issue and, all over the United States, parents began to suspect their children's caretakers. Allegations, trials, and convictions ensued. Even those who were not convicted had to bear the shame and disgrace of being accused in the first place. Thus, while moral panics are rooted more in the imagination than in reality, their consequences can be substantial and very real.

13

Freda Adler

Sisters in Crime[1]
1975

Before the publication of Freda Adler's book *Sisters in Crime: The Rise of the New Female Criminal*, criminologists paid little or no attention to female criminality. Noting that female criminality was far less common than male criminality, early theorists started with the question "what is it about female criminals that makes them more like men?," suggesting that crime is masculine behavior. Therefore, sexuality became the main feature explaining women's criminality. That is, early treatments of the topic tended to attribute women's criminality to disturbances in their sexuality, whereas discussions of male criminality rarely implicated the perpetrator's sexuality (unless, of course, the topic had to do with sex crimes).

Published in 1975, *Sisters in Crime* was one among many feminist treatises published in numerous fields in the 1960s and '70s. Adler argued that there are essentially no biological differences between men and women that account for their differential involvement in crime. Instead, the essential factor accounting for the differences in men's and women's participation in crime had to do with differences in societal expectations of men and women. Girls, the saying went, were made of "sugar and spice and everything nice," while boys were made of "snakes and snails and puppy dog tails." This is not what the two sexes were "made of" by nature; but what they were "made into" by the gendered nature of their socialization. Boys were raised to be aggressive, competitive and mischievous, while girls were raised to be passive, compliant, and nurturing. Boys were raised to get into trouble; girls were raised to stay out of it. Though the idea that differing rates of criminal activity among the sexes is due to their socialization and not their biological make-up may seem obvious to those of us in Western society in the 21st century, it was not so obvious before the 1970s. In this sense, Adler's book was groundbreaking and historically significant.

Noting that crime rates among women were accelerating faster than crime rates among men, Adler further argued that the crime-gender differential was not only explained by gender-role socialization, but also by differential access to criminal opportunities. Here she employed **opportunity theory** developed by Richard Cloward and Lloyd Ohlin (1960).[2] Cloward and Ohlin suggest *that in understanding criminal behavior, we have to take into account whether the opportunities for crime exist.* Just as, at certain times in certain places, there may be a scarcity of legitimate opportunities in the form of jobs, there may be a scarcity of illegitimate opportunities in the form of crime. In areas where there is nothing to steal, for example, there are likely to be few acts of theft.

Adler introduced her version of opportunity theory as it applied to women and it is sometimes called **emancipation theory**. In the first half of the 20th century, with women largely confined to the home by gendered role expectations, they had little opportunity to engage in criminal activity. *With the women's movement and the emancipation of women, as women began to have more opportunities to move from the home to the workplace, women gained more opportunities to commit crime.* Such, she argued, is what happened during World War II. Men went off to war, women moved into the work force to replace them, and crime rates among women increased faster than those among men. When the men returned from the war and replaced the women, sending them home to be mothers and homemakers, the differences in the growth in crime rates diminished. Moving to the modern era, Adler states, "with the emancipation of women . . . . girls are involved in more drinking, stealing, gang activity and fighting—behavior in keeping with their adoption of male roles."[3]

The publication of *Sisters in Crime* caused quite a sensation. Adler became something of a celebrity, interviewed often by the news media, and appearing on television talk shows. While few criminologists would deny that Adler ushered in the new field of feminist criminology, her book was heavily criticized, even by feminists. Written in the midst of the women's movement, some critics were concerned that Adler's book legitimated conservative fears of the changing roles of women by suggesting that "women's liberation" would lead to more crime. Another criticism centered around the data. When *Sister's in Crime* was published—and since—crime rates among women were indeed accelerating faster than those among men; however, the absolute number of crimes committed by women was still only a small fraction of those committed by men; and, even though the proportion of women in the workplace today nearly equals that of men, changes in the rates of crime committed by women, relative to men, are hardly commensurate with changes in women's participation rates in the work force.

However, the data do not disprove Adler's theory because her work emphasizes *both* gender-role socialization *and* increased access to criminal opportunities. It is the interplay between the two that may give rise to increasing rates of female criminality. While women's increased access to legitimate opportunities over the past half century has increased their access to illegitimate opportunities, gender-role socialization has not changed as fast as women's participation on the work force.

As we see girls raised with traits traditionally assigned to the male role, crime rates among women, relative to those among men, could begin to rise faster than they have been. This could be even more likely because as women are being raised to be more aggressive in roles outside of the home, it may be that men are being raised to be more nurturing in roles inside the home. These trends, *together with women's increased access to criminal opportunities*, could give credence to Adler's predictions.

While there may be a great deal of truth to Adler's insights, it is very difficult to predict future trends regarding the changing ratios of crime committed by the sexes. In any case, it was Freda Adler who played a pivotal role in the development of feminist criminology and who called our attention to the relationship between gender-role socialization and crime. According to criminologists Francis Cullen and Robert Agnew, Adler's "scholarship helped to ensure that no future generation of criminologists would ignore gender in the study of criminal behavior."[4]

14

Richard Quinney

Class, State, and Crime[1]
1977

With his earlier work focused on the differential treatment of white collar criminals versus street criminals, Richard Quinney turned his focus to the relationship between capitalism and crime. According to Marx (see Chapter 2), capitalism is an economic system whereby the labor of the working class is exploited by the elite class which owns and controls the means of production in society. The injustice inherent in such an unequal system of production necessitates the kind of force that can only be applied by the criminal justice system to maintain that system. *The criminal justice system, Quinney argues, was developed and is controlled by the elite class for the purpose of justifying and maintaining the unequal relations between the elite and the subjugated working class.* It is the elite's control of the criminal justice system that explains why behaviors perpetrated by the elite, the corporate elite in particular, that, while they may be injurious to vast numbers of people, are not defined as "criminal." Or, if they are considered criminal, their perpetrators are treated less severely than poor people who commit crime.

Take climate change for example. Weather conditions are becoming more extreme throughout much of the world, ocean levels are rising, vector-borne diseases are shifting their geographic boundaries. Thousands of people have already been displaced by climate catastrophes; hundreds of thousands more will be displaced by rising ocean levels. It could be that the whole of humankind will be adversely affected by the end of the century. Untold numbers could lose their livelihoods, even their lives as a result of climate change. What crimes committed by working class people could wreak this much devastation?

There are few among thousands of scientists who argue that corporate emissions do not significantly contribute to climate change. Those few that do are almost all on corporate payrolls. The corporate elite have marshalled forces—namely through political campaign contributions and through their influence on mass media—to effectively deny the reality of climate change. James Hansen, the Director of NASA's Institute for Space Studies who first alerted the public to the potential devastation of global warming in 1988, says the CEOs of major fossil fuel companies "should be tried for high crimes against humanity and nature."[2] Instead, they reap millions in salaries and stock options and, meanwhile, the prisons in the United States and in other capitalist countries are filled almost entirely with poor people. Quinney would argue that such injustices are due to the fact that the elite class is able to use the criminal justice system to defend its own interests at the expense of the working class. This applies not only to the law, but to the state itself. Quinney writes,

> The state exists as a device for controlling the exploited class, the class that labors, for the benefit of the ruling class. . . . Contrary to conventional wisdom, law instead of representing community custom is an instrument of the state that serves the interests of the developing capitalist ruling class.[3]

Based on the perpetrators' relationship to the means of capitalist production, Quinney lays out a typology of criminal activity. *Those crimes committed by the ruling elite, or on behalf of their interests, he calls* **crimes of domination**. This category includes crimes of control, crimes of government and crimes of economic domination. **Crimes of control** *are those carried out by agents of the criminal justice system in the name of law*, such as police brutality and the denial of the civil rights of the accused. **Crimes of government** *are those committed by elected and appointed government officials*, such as taking bribes or permitting torture in the name of national security. *And* **crimes of economic domination** *are those committed by the corporate elite for the purpose of furthering the accumulation of capital*, such as price fixing, insider trading and environmental pollution. The activities of the CEOs of fossil fuel companies that contribute to global warming and obstruct its remediation (mentioned above), though not considered "crimes" by the ruling elite, would fall into this latter category.

Quinney calls the crimes committed overwhelmingly by members of the working class **crimes of accommodation and resistance**. These are crimes that are a reaction to the conditions of exploitation, unemployment, and poverty that are endemic to capitalism. Crimes of accommodation include predatory crimes and personal crimes. **Predatory crimes** are parasitical in nature and are oriented toward financial gain, such as burglary, robbery and drug peddling. These are crimes that threaten the capitalist order because its participants are not engaged in capitalist production and such crimes demonstrate that wealth can be gained in activities that do not contribute to the interests of the ruling elite. **Personal crimes** are committed by poor people against poor people, such as murder, assault, and rape. These are acts of frustration committed by people "who have already been brutalized by the conditions of capitalism."[4] Lastly, **crimes of resistance** are "direct reflections of the alienation of labor."[5] According to Marx, all members of the working class are alienated from their work because they are paid less than what they are worth and the profits from their labor go to their employers, thereby increasing their employers' wealth and power and enabling them to further exploit their workers. Crimes of resistance include sabotage and organizing illegal strikes. Quinney argues that there will be more such crimes of resistance in the future because "increased economic growth necessitates the kind of labor that further alienates workers from their needs."[6] Indeed, in the modern economy, as digital automation is replacing workers throughout the workforce, job security has become more and more tenuous, thereby increasing employers' leverage over their employees. Increased alienation is the likely result.

Thus, Quinney is notable among a number of criminologists who employ Marxist theory to explain the relationship between poverty, unemployment, and crime in capitalist societies. Like other criminologists in the Marxist tradition, Quinney examines the role of power in the definition and treatment of crime. In the conflict between the haves and the have-nots, those with power have the ability to define crime in such a way as to further the interests of the powerful. Those without power are the victims of an unjust system and find themselves impoverished and often incarcerated. As wealth and power concentrate in fewer and fewer hands, the legitimacy of such a system becomes increasingly difficult to sustain and, therefore, many Marxist thinkers expect either that capitalism will fall, or the state will become increasingly repressive.

15

Lawrence Cohen and Marcus Felson

Routine Activities Theory
1979

Writing in the late 1970s, Lawrence Cohen and Marcus Felson[1] addressed their work to the apparent paradox between improving indicators of societal well-being and rising crime rates. Crime rates in the United States had been going up rather dramatically since the early 1960s and, yet, by the end of the 1970s, problems frequently associated with crime—such as unemployment, median family incomes for both black families and white families, and the percentage of kids dropping out of high school—had been improving. Even the most prominent explanation for rising crime rates—the growth in the proportion of males in their crime prone years (ages 15 to 24)4—was losing its relevance as this growth began to level off as the baby boom played itself out. Yet crime rates continued to climb.

Cohen and Felson attributed the rising crime rates to broader social changes taking place since the end of World War II that affected the **routine activities** of everyday American life. They argued that,

Structural changes in *routine activity patterns* can influence crime rates by affecting the convergence in space and time of the three minimal elements of direct-contact predatory violations: (1) *motivated offenders*, (2) *suitable targets*, and (3*) the absence of capable guardians*. . .[2]

When these three elements converge, crime is more likely. If any of these elements is missing, crime is far less likely. Unlike other criminological theories which often focused on the criminal's motivation, Cohen and Felson took the element of "motivated offenders" as a given, and focused their attention on "suitable targets" and the "absence of capable guardians."

Crime is more likely to occur when there is an absence of capable guardians. *In the decades following World War II, routine activities shifted away from the home. Increasing numbers of women left the home and went into the workplace and higher numbers of young women went off to college. These trends left more households unattended, without capable guardianship.* "Daily work activities," Cohen and Felson write, "separate many people from those they trust and the property they value."[3] In the 1960s and '70s, the proportion of people living alone began to climb as people waited longer to marry and as divorce rates rose. The higher proportion of single-adult households increased the likelihood that homes would be left unattended. Increased automobile ownership meant people could leave the house often and travel longer distances for longer intervals. Victories in collective bargaining meant more time off from work and more vacations away from home. Not surprisingly, as routine activities shifted away from the home, burglary rates climbed faster than rates for most other categories of crime.

Changes in production and technology also changed routine activities, especially with regard to both guardianship and suitable targets. As leisure time was increasing in the 1960s and '70s people were purchasing more electronics to fill that time with entertainment, more televisions, more radios, more stereos, etc. So while guardianship was compromised by more people working and away on vacations, when people were not at work or away on vacations, more of them were home at night watching television and listening to music. This reduced the number of people who were out at night communing with their neighbors. This reduced "natural surveillance," or the number of capable guardians keeping an eye out for trouble and deterring criminal activities. Motivated offenders could violate the law away from public scrutiny.

A society so dependent on mass consumption inevitably produces massive quantities of suitable targets. More importantly, technological innovation was making these devices smaller, lighter, and more portable—things more easily removed from unattended homes by motivated offenders.

While Cohen and Felson took the element of motivated offenders for granted, we might surmise based on the data and the literature, young people fall disproportionately into this category. Their routine activities are generally less structured than those of their adult counterparts, especially when they are out of school. And while we should be careful when we infer that this category of people are more motivated to commit crime, it may be safer to say that teenagers are often motivated to absent themselves from capable guardianship, which increases the likelihood of a convergence among motivated offenders, suitable targets, and an absence of capable guardians.

Cohen and Felson admit the theory of routine activities is hardly new. We see elements of opportunity theory (see Chapter 13) in that the presence of suitable targets and the absence of capable guardians create the opportunity for crime. We also see some elements of control theory (see Chapter 11) in that the motivation to commit crime is assumed and a good deal of the focus is on a lack of controls on the offender or his/her environment (i.e. lack of capable guardians.) However, Cohen and Felson should be credited with bringing a together a disparate body of literature on how crime rates are affected by social change and changing lifestyles under the umbrella of routine activities theory.

Notes

Introduction

[1] Henry Paolucci in his introduction to Beccaria's *On Crimes and Punishments*. Bobb-Merrill, 1963, p. xi.

Chapter 1: Cesare Beccaria

[1] Cesare Beccaria, *On Crimes and Punishments*, translated by Henry Paolucci. Indianapolis: Bobbs-Merrill, 1963.

[2] Elio Monachesi, "Cesare Beccaria," from *Pioneers in Criminology*, 2nd edition, edited by Hermann Mannheim. Montclair, NJ: Patterson Smith, 1972, p. 36.

[2] *On Crimes and Punishments*, pp. 42-43.

[3] What is being referred to in this figure as "the government" Hobbes called "the sovereign." While there are differences in meaning, "the government" better serves our purposes in understanding Beccaria's work.

[4] *On Crimes and Punishments*, pp. 42-43. Emphasis added.

[5] Ibid., p. 43. Emphasis added.

[6] Ibid., p. 58.

[7] Ibid., p. 30.

[8] Henry Paolucci, Introduction to *On Crimes and Punishments*. Indianapolis: Bobbs-Merrill, 1963, p. xi.

[9] Ibid., quoting a 1952 passage from Harry Elmer Barnes' and Howard Becker's *Social Thought from Lore to Science*.

Chapter 2: Karl Marx

[1] Karl Marx, *Das Kapital*, translated by Samuel Moore and Edward Aveling, Gateway Edition Reprint Series. Skeptical Reader, 1996.

[2] Steven Spitzer, "Toward a Marxian Theory of Deviance," *Social Problems*, vol. 22, no. 5, June 1975.

[3] Edwin Sutherland, Presidential address to the American Sociological Association in 1940. Then he published *White Collar Crime*, New York: Dryden, 1949.

Chapter 3: Emile Durkheim

[1] Emile Durkheim, *The Rules of the Sociological Method,* translated by S. Soloway and J.H. Mueller, edited by G. Catlin. Chicago: University of Chicago Press, 1938.

[2] Francis A.J. Ianni, "Ethnic Succession in Organized Crime: Summary Report," Law Enforcement Assistance Administration, U.S. Department of Justice, December 1973.

[3] Ibid.

[4] Kai Erikson, *Wayward Puritans*. New York: Macmillan. 1966.

Chapter 4: Social Disorganization Theory

[1] Thomas, W. & F. Znaniecki. (1920). *The Polish Peasant in Europe & America*, vol. 4. Boston: Gorham.

[2] Thorsten Sellin, *Culture Conflict and Crime*, Bulletin No. 41, (New York: Social Science Research Council), 1938, p. 63.

[3] Clifford Shaw and Henry Mckay, *Juvenile Delinquency and Urban Areas*. 1942. Reprinted in *The Chicago School of Criminology 1914-1945,* Piers Beirne, editor, Routledge, 2006, p. 168. Emphasis added.

[4] James Bennett, *Oral History and Delinquency: The Rhetoric of Criminology*. Chicago: University of Chicago Press, 1981,. P. 170.

[5] Wilson, James Q., Kelling, George L. (Mar 1982), "Broken Windows: The police and neighborhood safety", *The Atlantic*. http://www.theatlantic.com/magazine/archive/1982/03/brok en-windows/304465/

Chapter 5: Robert Merton

[1] Robert Merton, "Social Structure and Anomie," *American Sociological Review*, vol. 3, 1938, pp. 672–682.

[2] Francis Cullen and Steven Messner, "The Making of Criminology Revisited: An Oral History of Merton's Anomie Paradigm," from *The Origins of American Criminology, Advances in Criminological Theory*, Volume 16, Francis Cullen,

Sheryl Lero Jonson, Andrew Myer, and Freda Adler, editors. Transaction Publishers, 2011.

[3] Emile Durkheim, *Suicide: A Study in Sociology*, translated by John Spaulding and George Simpson, edited by George Simpson. The Free Press, 1951.

Chapter 6: Edwin Sutherland

[1] Edwin Sutherland and Donald Cressey, *Principles of Criminology*, 7th edition. Philadelphia: J.B. Lippincott, 1966.

[2] Ibid.,, p. 81.

[3] Ibid.

[4] Ibid., p. 82.

[5] Edwin H. Sutherland; Donald Cressey and David Luckenbill, Principles of Criminology, 11th edition. AltaMira Press, 1992, p. 89.

[6] Howard W. Odum, *American Sociology: The Story of Sociology in the United States through 1950*. Quoted on the American Sociological Associations web page: http://www.asanet.org/ about/presidents/Edwin_Sutherland.cfm.

[7] Donald Cressey, "The Poverty of Theory in Corporate Crime Research," from *Advances in Criminological Theory*, Volume 1. Willima Laufer and Freda Adler, editors. Transaction Publishers, 1987, p. 37.

Chapter 7: Albert Cohen

[1] Albert Cohen, *Delinquent Boys: The Culture of the Gang*. Glencoe, IL: The Free Press, 1955.

[2] Ibid., p. 28.

Chapter 8: Gresham Sykes

[1] Gresham Sykes and David Matza, "Techniques of Neutralization: A Theory of Delinquency," *American Sociological Review*, vol. 22, 1957, pp. 664-670.

[2] Gresham Sykes, *The Society of Captives: A Study of a Maximum Security Prison*. Princeton University Press, 1958.

[3] Michael Reisig, "The Champion, the Contender, and the Challenger: Top Ranked Books in Prison Studies." *The Prison Journal*, vol. 81, 2001, pp. 389-407.

Chapter 9: Labeling Theory
[1] Charles Horton Cooley, *Human Nature and the Social Order*. Scribner's, 1902.

[2] George Herbert Mead, *Mind, Self and Society: From the Standpoint of a Social Behaviorist*, edited by Charles Morris. University of Chicago Press, 1954. (Original work published 1934.) See also Herbert Blumer, *Symbolic Interactionism: Perspective and Method*. Prentice-Hall, 1969.

[3] Edwin Lemert, "Secondary Deviance and Role Conceptions," from *Social Deviance*, edited by Ronald Farrell and Victoria Lynn Swigert. New York: J.B. Lippencott, 1978, pp. 94-97. (Original work published 1951).

[4] Frank Tannenbaum, "Definition and the Dramatization of Evil," from *Deviance Across Cultures: Constructions of Difference*, 2nd edition, edited by Robert Heiner. New York: Oxford University Press, 2014, p. 57. (Tannenbaum wrote this in 1938, long before "labeling theory" entered the lexicon.)

[5] Ibid.

[6] David F. Musto, *The American Disease: Origins of Narcotic Control*. New York: Oxford University Press, 1987, p. 244. See also Troy Duster, "The Legislation of Morality: Creating Drug Laws," in D. H. Kelly (ed.), *Deviant Behavior,* 3rd ed. New York: St. Martin's, 1989, 29–39.

Chapter 10: Joseph Gusfield
[1] Joseph Gusfield, *Symbolic Crusade: Status Politics and the American Temperance Movement*. Urbana: University of Illinois Press, 1963.

Chapter 11: Travis Hirschi
[1] Travis Hirschi, *The Causes of Delinquency*. Berkeley, University of California Press, 1969.

[2] Ibid., p. 22.
[3] Ibid., p. 25.

Chapter 12: Stanley Cohen
[1] Stanley Cohen, *Folks Devils and Moral Panics: The Creation of the Mods and Rockers*. London: MacGibbon and Kee, 1972.
[2] Cohen was actually born and raised in South Africa, but trained and conducted most of his work in England.
[3] Ibid., p. 29.
[4] Kenneth Thompson, "The Classic Moral Panic," from *Deviance Across Cultures*, 2nd edition, edited by Robert Heiner. New York: Oxford University Press, 2014.
[5] Ibid.
[6] Vintage television news report posted on YouTube, https://www.youtube.com/watch?v=5Rj-OHCusEI.
[7] Cohen, *Folk Devils and Moral Panics*, p. 45.
[8] Thompson, "The Classic Moral Panic," p. 120.
[9] Jeffrey Victor, *Satanic Panic: The Creation of a Contemporary Legend*. Chicago: Open Court, 1993.
[10] Mary DeYoung, "The Devil Goes to Day Care: McMartin and the Making of a Moral Panic," from *Deviance Across Cultures*, 2nd edition, edited by Robert Heiner. New York: Oxford University Press, 2014, p. 125. Emphasis added.

Chapter 13: Freda Adler
[1] Freda Adler, *Sisters in Crime: The Rise of the New Female Criminal*. McGraw Hill, 1975.
[2] Richard Cloward and Lloyd Ohlin, *Delinquency and Opportunity*. Glencoe, IL: Free Press, 1960.
[3] *Sisters in Crime*, p. 95.
[4] Francis Cullen and Robert Agnew, *Criminological Theory: Past and Present*. Los Angeles: Roxbury, 2003, p. 405.

Chapter 14: Richard Quinney
[1] Richard Quinney, *Class State and Crime: On the Theory and Practice of Criminal Justice*. New York: Longman, 1977.

[2] "James Hansen: "Try Fossil Fuel CEOs For 'High Crimes Against Humanity,'" *Environmental Leader*, June 24, 2008. http://www.environmentalleader.com/2008/06/24/james-hansen-try-fossil-fuel-ceos-for-high-crimes-against-humanity/#ixzz3ihAu45zL.

[3] *Class State, and Crime*, p. 45.

[4] Ibid., p. 54.

[5] Ibid., p. 55.

[6] Ibid.

Chapter 15: Lawrence Cohen and Marcus Felson

[1] Lawrence E. Cohen and Marcus Felson, "Social Change and Crime Rate Trends: A Routine Activity Approach," *American Sociological Review*, vol. 44 (1979), pp. 588-608.

[2] Ibid., p. 589. Emphasis added.

[3] Ibid., p. 591.